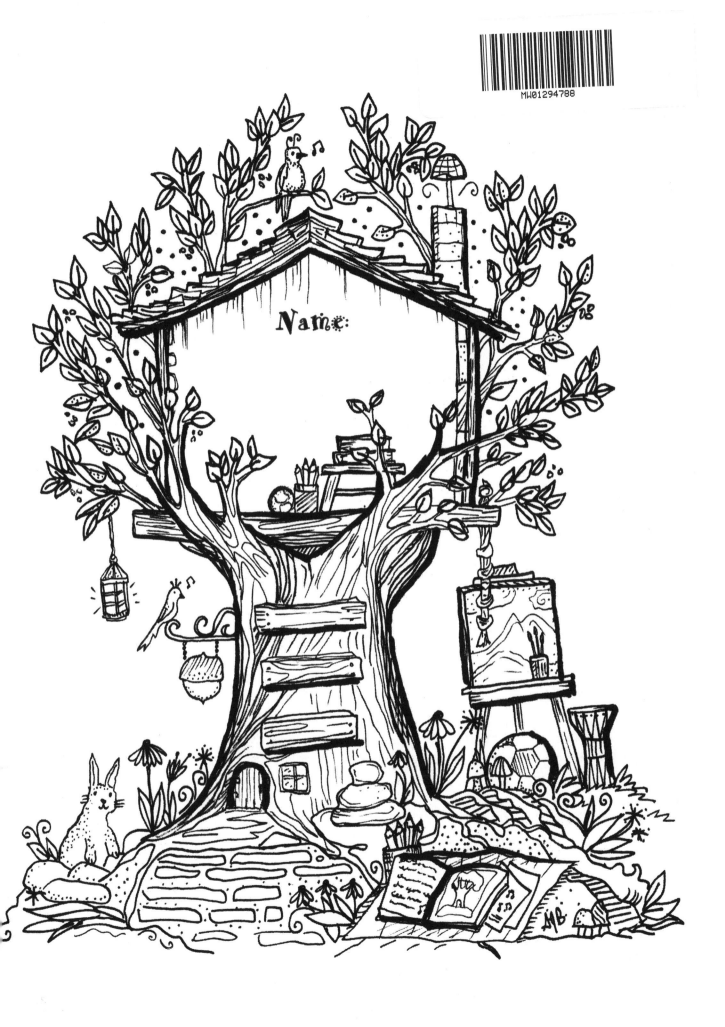

The Thinking Tree
Do-IT-Yourself Homeschooling
READING TIME

Sarah Janisse Brown

Copyright 2020
The Thinking Tree, LLC
FunSchooling.com

Instructions:
Use one page each day, for 180 days,
accompanied by the books of your choice.
Follow the prompts on each page to create a portfolio
of your library based learning experience.

Supplies: Thesaurus, Dictionary,
And Reading Materials Fiction and Non-Fiction.

My Reading Time Book List

Book Title: Date:

Date

Book

Author: _____

Genre: _____

Illustrator: _____

Theme: _____

_____

Subject: _____
Setting: _____

Favorite Part:

_____
_____
_____

Rating:
AWFUL
BAD
LAME
BORING
OKAY
NICE
GOOD
GREAT
SUPER
AMAZING

Draw or Copy an Illustration From Your Book:

Reading Time

Draw or Write About Four interesting Things From Your Book

Title:_____

Date:_____

Date

Book

Author: _____

Genre: _____

Illustrator: _____

Theme: _____

_____

Subject: _____
Setting: _____

Favorite Part:

_____
_____
_____

Rating:
AWFUL
BAD
LAME
BORING
OKAY
NICE
GOOD
GREAT
SUPER
AMAZING

Draw or Copy an Illustration From Your Book:

Reading Time

Draw or Write About Four interesting Things From Your Book

Title:_____

Date:_____

Date

Book

Author: _____

Genre: _____

Illustrator: _____

Theme: _____

_____

Subject: _____
Setting: _____

Favorite Part:

_____
_____
_____

Rating:
AWFUL
BAD
LAME
BORING
OKAY
NICE
GOOD
GREAT
SUPER
AMAZING

Draw or Copy an Illustration From Your Book:

Words, Words, Words.

Write down ten words you liked from your reading time. Using a thesaurus, look up related words and write them down too.

Thesaurus Words

WORD OF THE DAY:
What was your favorite word today and why?

Date

Book

Author: _____

Genre: _____

Illustrator: _____

Theme: _____

_____

Subject:_____
Setting:_____

Favorite Part:
_____
_____
_____

Rating:
AWFUL
BAD
LAME
BORING
OKAY
NICE
GOOD
GREAT
SUPER
AMAZING

Draw or Copy an Illustration From Your Book:

Reading Time

Draw or Write About Four interesting Things From Your Book

Title:_____

Date:_____

Choose your favorite book to focus on today. Choose a section to copy and after you're done, read it aloud seven times.

Title_____ Page Number_____

Story Board & Comics

Create a story board or comic strip based on
your favorite book from this week.

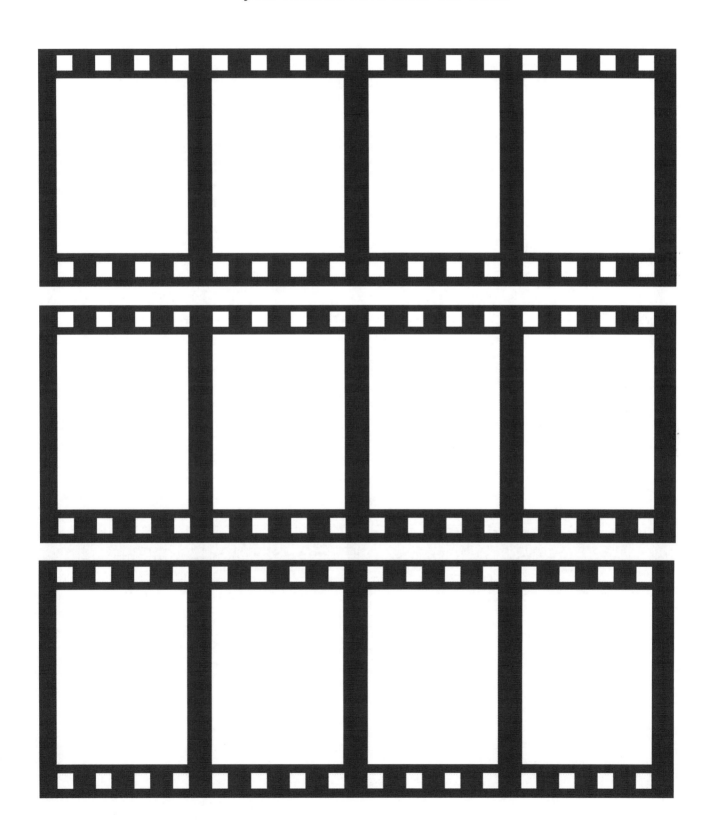

Journaling & Creative Writing

Date

Book

Author: _____

Genre: _____

Illustrator: _____

Theme: _____

_____

Subject: _____
Setting: _____

Favorite Part:

_____
_____
_____

Rating:
AWFUL
BAD
LAME
BORING
OKAY
NICE
GOOD
GREAT
SUPER
AMAZING

Draw or Copy an Illustration From Your Book:

Reading Time

Draw or Write About Four interesting Things From Your Book

Title:_____

Date:_____

Date

Book

Author: _____

Genre: _____

Illustrator: _____

Theme: _____

_____

Subject: _____
Setting: _____

Favorite Part:

_____
_____
_____

Rating:
AWFUL
BAD
LAME
BORING
OKAY
NICE
GOOD
GREAT
SUPER
AMAZING

Draw or Copy an Illustration From Your Book:

Reading Time

Draw or Write About Four interesting Things From Your Book

Title:_____

Date:_____

Date
_____

Book

Author: _____

Genre: _____

Illustrator: _____

Theme: _____

_____

Subject: _____
Setting: _____

Favorite Part:

_____
_____
_____

Rating:
AWFUL
BAD
LAME
BORING
OKAY
NICE
GOOD
GREAT
SUPER
AMAZING

Draw or Copy an Illustration From Your Book:

Words, Words, Words.

Write down ten words you liked from your reading time.
Using a thesaurus, look up related words and write them down too.

Thesaurus Words

_____   _____
_____   _____
_____   _____
_____   _____
_____   _____
_____   _____
_____   _____
_____   _____
_____   _____
_____   _____

WORD OF THE DAY:
What was your favorite word today and why?

_____
_____
_____

Date

_____

Book

Author: _____

Genre: _____

Illustrator: _____

Theme: _____

_____

Subject: _____
Setting: _____

Favorite Part:

_____
_____
_____

Rating:
AWFUL
BAD
LAME
BORING
OKAY
NICE
GOOD
GREAT
SUPER
AMAZING

Draw or Copy an Illustration From Your Book:

Reading Time

Draw or Write About Four interesting Things From Your Book

Title:_____

Date:_____

Book of the Week

Choose your favorite book to focus on today. Choose a section to copy and after you're done, read it aloud seven times.

Title_____ Page Number_____

Story Board & Comics

Create a story board or comic strip based on
your favorite book from this week.

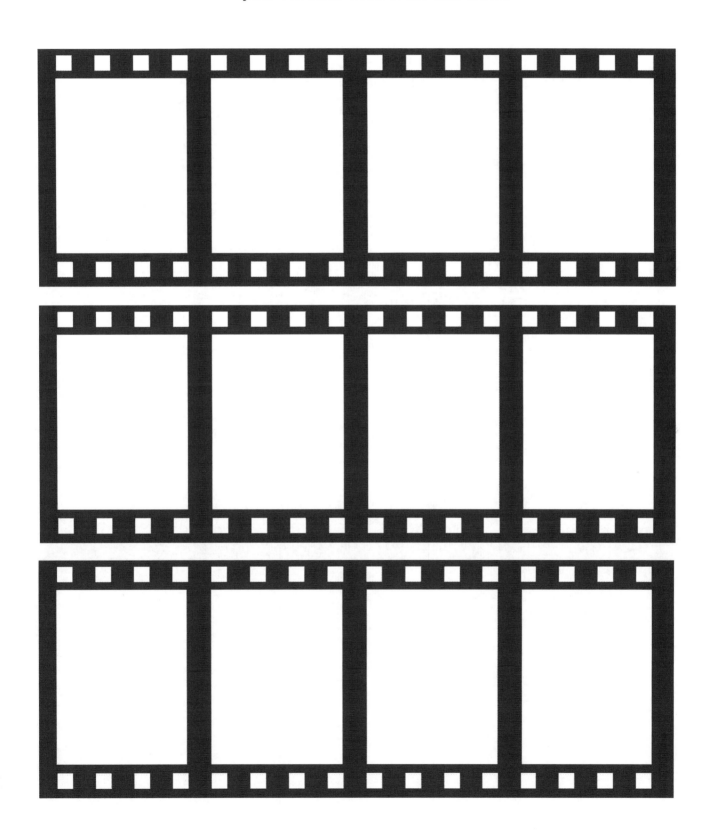

Journaling & Creative Writing

Date

Book

Author: _____

Genre: _____

Illustrator: _____

Theme: _____

_____

Subject: _____
Setting: _____

Favorite Part:

_____
_____
_____

Rating:
AWFUL
BAD
LAME
BORING
OKAY
NICE
GOOD
GREAT
SUPER
AMAZING

Draw or Copy an Illustration From Your Book:

Reading Time

Draw or Write About Four interesting Things From Your Book

Title:_____

Date:_____

Date

Book

Author: _____

Genre: _____

Illustrator: _____

Theme: _____

_____

Subject: _____
Setting: _____

Favorite Part:
_____
_____
_____

Rating:
AWFUL
BAD
LAME
BORING
OKAY
NICE
GOOD
GREAT
SUPER
AMAZING

Draw or Copy an Illustration From Your Book:

Reading Time

Draw or Write About Four interesting Things From Your Book

Title:_____

Date:_____

Date

Book

Author: _____

Genre: _____

Illustrator: _____

Theme: _____

_____

Subject: _____
Setting: _____

Favorite Part:

_____
_____
_____

Rating:
AWFUL
BAD
LAME
BORING
OKAY
NICE
GOOD
GREAT
SUPER
AMAZING

Draw or Copy an Illustration From Your Book:

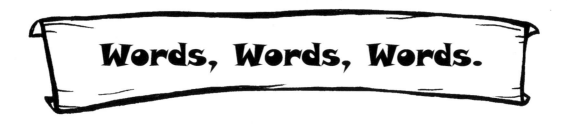

Words, Words, Words.

Write down ten words you liked from your reading time.
Using a thesaurus, look up related words and write them down too.

Thesaurus Words

_____   _____
_____   _____
_____   _____
_____   _____
_____   _____
_____   _____
_____   _____
_____   _____
_____   _____
_____   _____

WORD OF THE DAY:
What was your favorite word today and why?
_____
_____

Date

Book

Author: _____

Genre: _____

Illustrator: _____

Theme: _____

_____

Subject: _____
Setting: _____

Favorite Part:

_____
_____
_____

Rating:
AWFUL
BAD
LAME
BORING
OKAY
NICE
GOOD
GREAT
SUPER
AMAZING

Draw or Copy an Illustration From Your Book:

Reading Time

Draw or Write About Four interesting Things From Your Book

Title:_____

Date:_____

Book of the Week

Choose your favorite book to focus on today. Choose a section to copy and after you're done, read it aloud seven times.

Title_____ Page Number_____

Story Board & Comics

Create a story board or comic strip based on your favorite book from this week.

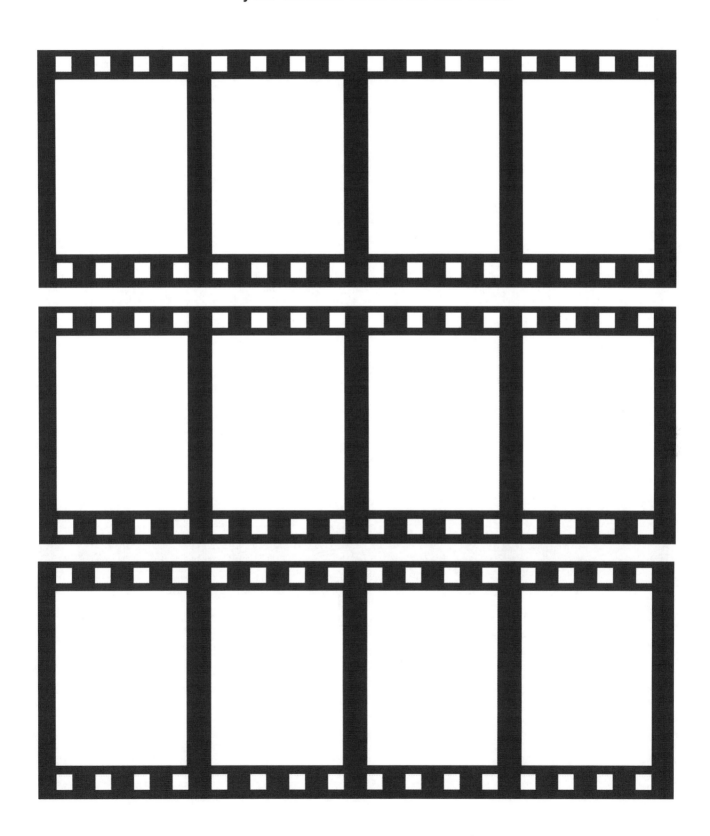

Journaling & Creative Writing

Date

Book

Author: _____

Genre: _____

Illustrator: _____

Theme: _____

_____

Subject: _____
Setting: _____

Favorite Part:

_____
_____
_____

Rating:
AWFUL
BAD
LAME
BORING
OKAY
NICE
GOOD
GREAT
SUPER
AMAZING

Draw or Copy an Illustration From Your Book:

Reading Time

Draw or Write About Four interesting Things From Your Book

Title:_____

Date:_____

Date

Book

Author: _____

Genre: _____

Illustrator: _____

Theme: _____

_____

Subject: _____
Setting: _____

Favorite Part:
_____
_____
_____

Rating:
AWFUL
BAD
LAME
BORING
OKAY
NICE
GOOD
GREAT
SUPER
AMAZING

Draw or Copy an Illustration From Your Book:

Reading Time

Draw or Write About Four interesting Things From Your Book

Title:_____

Date:_____

Date

Book

Author: _____

Genre: _____

Illustrator: _____

Theme: _____

_____

Subject: _____
Setting: _____

Favorite Part:

_____
_____
_____

Rating:
AWFUL
BAD
LAME
BORING
OKAY
NICE
GOOD
GREAT
SUPER
AMAZING

Draw or Copy an Illustration From Your Book:

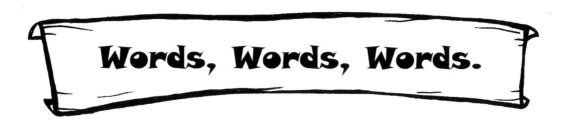

Words, Words, Words.

Write down ten words you liked from your reading time.
Using a thesaurus, look up related words and write them down too.

Thesaurus Words

WORD OF THE DAY:
What was your favorite word today and why?

Date

Book

Author: _____

Genre: _____

Illustrator: _____

Theme: _____

_____

Subject: _____
Setting: _____

Favorite Part:

_____
_____
_____

Rating:
AWFUL
BAD
LAME
BORING
OKAY
NICE
GOOD
GREAT
SUPER
AMAZING

Draw or Copy an Illustration From Your Book:

Reading Time

Draw or Write About Four interesting Things From Your Book

Title:_____

Date:_____

Book of the Week

Choose your favorite book to focus on today. Choose a section to copy and after you're done, read it aloud seven times.

Title_____ Page Number_____

Story Board & Comics

Create a story board or comic strip based on
your favorite book from this week.

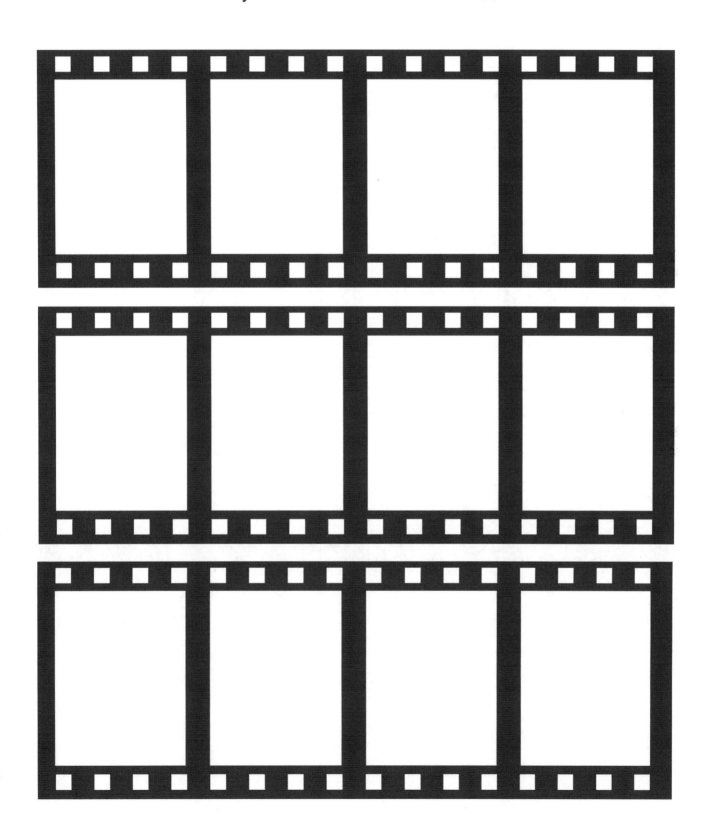

Journaling & Creative Writing

Date

Book

Author: _____

Genre: _____

Illustrator: _____

Theme: _____

_____

Subject: _____
Setting: _____

Favorite Part:

_____
_____
_____

Rating:
AWFUL
BAD
LAME
BORING
OKAY
NICE
GOOD
GREAT
SUPER
AMAZING

Draw or Copy an Illustration From Your Book:

Reading Time

Draw or Write About Four interesting Things From Your Book

Title:_____

Date:_____

Date

Book

Author: _____

Genre: _____

Illustrator: _____

Theme: _____

_____

Subject: _____
Setting: _____

Favorite Part:
_____
_____
_____

Rating:
AWFUL
BAD
LAME
BORING
OKAY
NICE
GOOD
GREAT
SUPER
AMAZING

Draw or Copy an Illustration From Your Book:

Reading Time

Draw or Write About Four interesting Things From Your Book

Title:_____

Date:_____

Date

Book

Author: _____

Genre: _____

Illustrator: _____

Theme: _____

_____

Subject: _____
Setting: _____

Favorite Part:

_____
_____
_____

Rating:
AWFUL
BAD
LAME
BORING
OKAY
NICE
GOOD
GREAT
SUPER
AMAZING

Draw or Copy an Illustration From Your Book:

Words, Words, Words.

Write down ten words you liked from your reading time.
Using a thesaurus, look up related words and write them down too.

Thesaurus Words

_____   _____
_____   _____
_____   _____
_____   _____
_____   _____
_____   _____
_____   _____
_____   _____
_____   _____
_____   _____
_____   _____
_____   _____

WORD OF THE DAY:
What was your favorite word today and why?
_____
_____

Date
_____

Book

Author: _____

Genre: _____

Illustrator: _____

Theme: _____

_____

Subject: _____
Setting: _____

Favorite Part:

_____
_____
_____

Rating:
AWFUL
BAD
LAME
BORING
OKAY
NICE
GOOD
GREAT
SUPER
AMAZING

Draw or Copy an Illustration From Your Book:

Reading Time

Draw or Write About Four interesting Things From Your Book

Title:_____

Date:_____

Book of the Week

Choose your favorite book to focus on today. Choose a section to copy and after you're done, read it aloud seven times.

Title_____ Page Number_____

Story Board & Comics

Create a story board or comic strip based on your favorite book from this week.

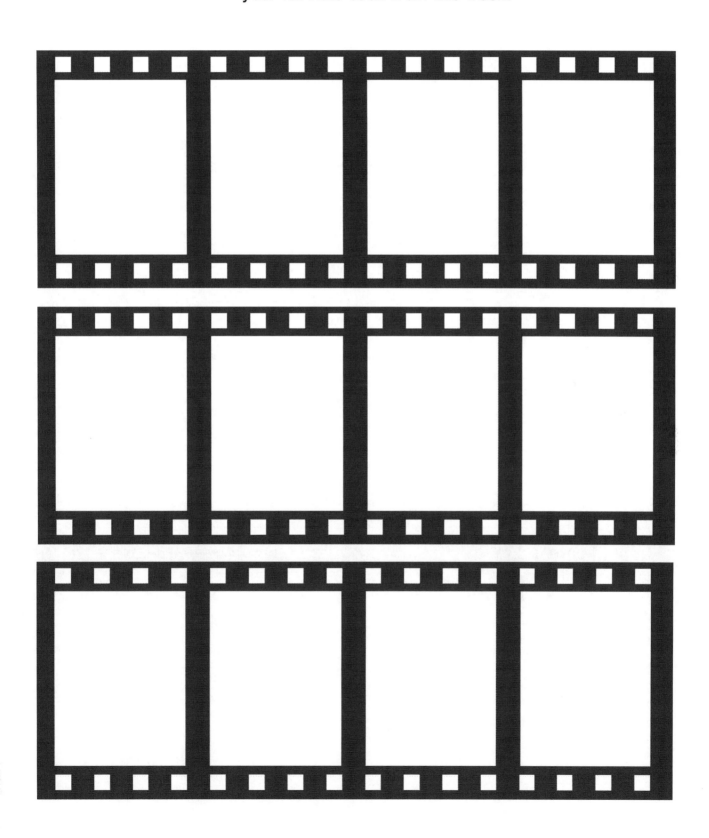

Journaling & Creative Writing

Date

Book

Author: _____

Genre: _____

Illustrator: _____

Theme: _____

_____

Subject: _____
Setting: _____

Favorite Part:

_____
_____
_____

Rating:
AWFUL
BAD
LAME
BORING
OKAY
NICE
GOOD
GREAT
SUPER
AMAZING

Draw or Copy an Illustration From Your Book:

Reading Time

Draw or Write About Four interesting Things From Your Book

Title:_____

Date:_____

Date

Book

Author: _____

Genre: _____

Illustrator: _____

Theme: _____

_____

Subject: _____
Setting: _____

Favorite Part:

_____
_____
_____

Rating:
AWFUL
BAD
LAME
BORING
OKAY
NICE
GOOD
GREAT
SUPER
AMAZING

Draw or Copy an Illustration From Your Book:

Reading Time

Draw or Write About Four interesting Things From Your Book

Title:_____

Date:_____

Date

Book

Author: _____

Genre: _____

Illustrator: _____

Theme: _____

_____

Subject: _____
Setting: _____

Favorite Part:

_____
_____
_____

Rating:
AWFUL
BAD
LAME
BORING
OKAY
NICE
GOOD
GREAT
SUPER
AMAZING

Draw or Copy an Illustration From Your Book:

Words, Words, Words.

Write down ten words you liked from your reading time.
Using a thesaurus, look up related words and write them down too.

Thesaurus Words

WORD OF THE DAY:
What was your favorite word today and why?

Date

Book

Author: _____

Genre: _____

Illustrator: _____

Theme: _____
_____

Subject: _____
Setting: _____

Favorite Part:
_____
_____
_____

Rating:
AWFUL
BAD
LAME
BORING
OKAY
NICE
GOOD
GREAT
SUPER
AMAZING

Draw or Copy an Illustration From Your Book:

Reading Time

Draw or Write About Four interesting Things From Your Book

Title:_____

Date:_____

Journaling & Creative Writing

Date

Book

Author: _____

Genre: _____

Illustrator: _____

Theme: _____

_____

Subject: _____
Setting: _____

Favorite Part:
_____
_____
_____

Draw or Copy an Illustration From Your Book:

Rating:
AWFUL
BAD
LAME
BORING
OKAY
NICE
GOOD
GREAT
SUPER
AMAZING

Reading Time

Draw or Write About Four interesting Things From Your Book

Title:_____

Date:_____

Date
_____

Book

Author: _____

Genre: _____

Illustrator: _____

Theme: _____

_____

Subject: _____
Setting: _____

Favorite Part:

_____
_____
_____

Rating:
AWFUL
BAD
LAME
BORING
OKAY
NICE
GOOD
GREAT
SUPER
AMAZING

Draw or Copy an Illustration From Your Book:

Reading Time

Draw or Write About Four interesting Things From Your Book

Title:_____

Date:_____

Date

Book

Author: _____

Genre: _____

Illustrator: _____

Theme: _____

_____

Subject: _____
Setting: _____

Favorite Part:

_____
_____
_____

Rating:
AWFUL
BAD
LAME
BORING
OKAY
NICE
GOOD
GREAT
SUPER
AMAZING

Draw or Copy an Illustration From Your Book:

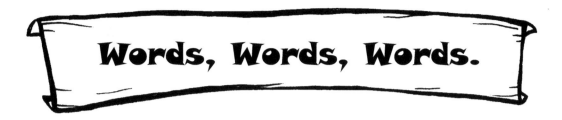

Words, Words, Words.

Write down ten words you liked from your reading time.
Using a thesaurus, look up related words and write them down too.

Thesaurus Words

_____   _____
_____   _____
_____   _____
_____   _____
_____   _____
_____   _____
_____   _____
_____   _____
_____   _____
_____   _____

WORD OF THE DAY:
What was your favorite word today and why?
_____
_____

Date

Book

Author: _____

Genre: _____

Illustrator: _____

Theme: _____

_____

Subject: _____
Setting: _____

Favorite Part:
_____
_____
_____

Rating:
AWFUL
BAD
LAME
BORING
OKAY
NICE
GOOD
GREAT
SUPER
AMAZING

Draw or Copy an Illustration From Your Book:

Reading Time

Draw or Write About Four interesting Things From Your Book

Title:_____

Date:_____

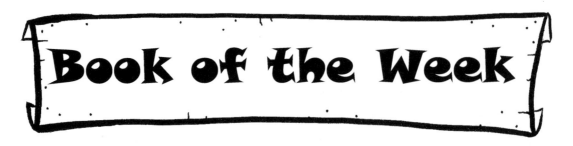

Book of the Week

Choose your favorite book to focus on today. Choose a section to copy and after you're done, read it aloud seven times.

Title_____ Page Number_____

Story Board & Comics

Create a story board or comic strip based on your favorite book from this week.

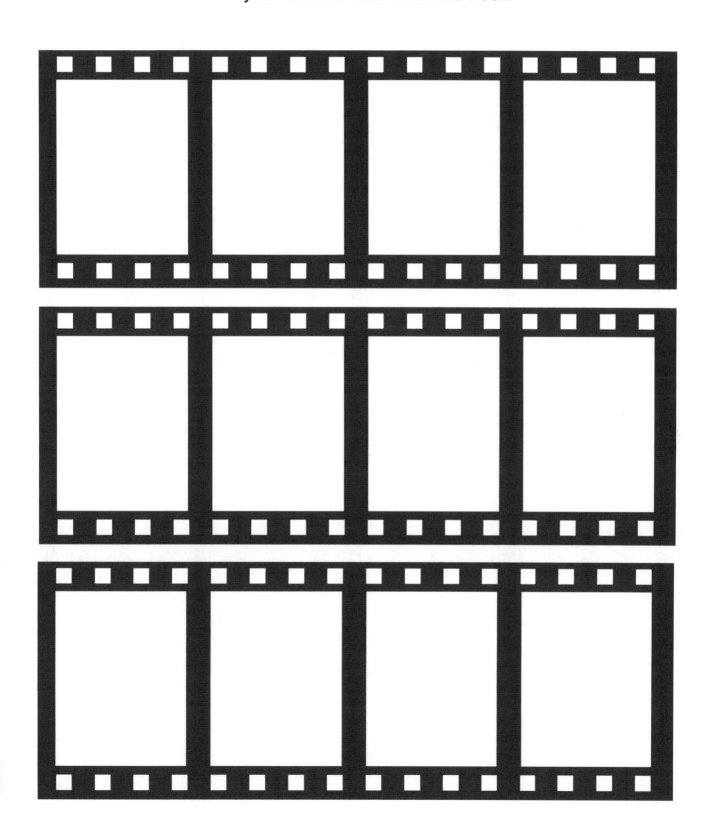

Journaling & Creative Writing

Date

Book

Author: _____

Genre:_____

Illustrator: _____

Theme: _____

_____

Subject:_____
Setting:_____

Favorite Part:

_____
_____
_____

Rating:
AWFUL
BAD
LAME
BORING
OKAY
NICE
GOOD
GREAT
SUPER
AMAZING

Draw or Copy an Illustration From Your Book:

Reading Time

Draw or Write About Four interesting Things From Your Book

Title:_____

Date:_____

Date

Book

Author: _____

Genre: _____

Illustrator: _____

Theme: _____

_____

Subject: _____
Setting: _____

Favorite Part:

_____
_____
_____

Rating:
AWFUL
BAD
LAME
BORING
OKAY
NICE
GOOD
GREAT
SUPER
AMAZING

Draw or Copy an Illustration From Your Book:

Reading Time

Draw or Write About Four interesting Things From Your Book

Title:_____

Date:_____

Date

Book

Author: _____

Genre: _____

Illustrator: _____

Theme: _____

_____

Subject: _____
Setting: _____

Favorite Part:

_____
_____
_____

Rating:
AWFUL
BAD
LAME
BORING
OKAY
NICE
GOOD
GREAT
SUPER
AMAZING

Draw or Copy an Illustration From Your Book:

Words, Words, Words.

Write down ten words you liked from your reading time.
Using a thesaurus, look up related words and write them down too.

Thesaurus Words

_____   _____
_____   _____
_____   _____
_____   _____
_____   _____
_____   _____
_____   _____
_____   _____
_____   _____
_____   _____

WORD OF THE DAY:
What was your favorite word today and why?
_____
_____
_____

Date

Book

Author: _____

Genre:_____

Illustrator: _____

Theme: _____

_____

Subject:_____
Setting:_____

Favorite Part:

_____
_____
_____

Rating:
AWFUL
BAD
LAME
BORING
OKAY
NICE
GOOD
GREAT
SUPER
AMAZING

Draw or Copy an Illustration From Your Book:

Reading Time

Draw or Write About Four interesting Things From Your Book

Title:_____

Date:_____

Book of the Week

Choose your favorite book to focus on today. Choose a section to copy and after you're done, read it aloud seven times.

Title_____ Page Number_____

Story Board & Comics

Create a story board or comic strip based on
your favorite book from this week.

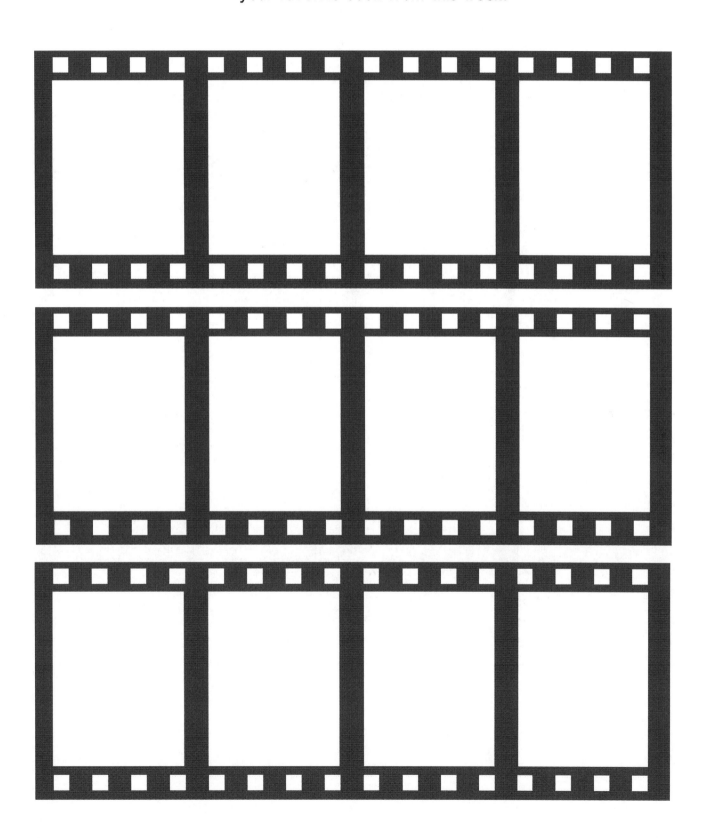

Journaling & Creative Writing

Date

Book

Author: _____

Genre: _____

Illustrator: _____

Theme: _____

_____

Subject: _____
Setting: _____

Favorite Part:

_____
_____
_____

Rating:
AWFUL
BAD
LAME
BORING
OKAY
NICE
GOOD
GREAT
SUPER
AMAZING

Draw or Copy an Illustration From Your Book:

Reading Time

Draw or Write About Four interesting Things From Your Book

Title:_____

Date:_____

Date

Book

Author: _____

Genre: _____

Illustrator: _____

Theme: _____

_____

Subject: _____
Setting: _____

Favorite Part:

_____
_____
_____

Rating:
AWFUL
BAD
LAME
BORING
OKAY
NICE
GOOD
GREAT
SUPER
AMAZING

Draw or Copy an Illustration From Your Book:

Reading Time

Draw or Write About Four interesting Things From Your Book
Title:_____
Date:_____

Date

Book

Author: _____

Genre: _____

Illustrator: _____

Theme: _____

_____

Subject: _____
Setting: _____

Favorite Part:
_____
_____
_____

Rating:
AWFUL
BAD
LAME
BORING
OKAY
NICE
GOOD
GREAT
SUPER
AMAZING

Draw or Copy an Illustration From Your Book:

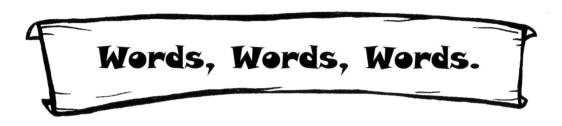

Words, Words, Words.

Write down ten words you liked from your reading time.
Using a thesaurus, look up related words and write them down too.

Thesaurus Words

WORD OF THE DAY:
What was your favorite word today and why?

Date

Book

Author: _____

Genre: _____

Illustrator: _____

Theme: _____

_____

Subject: _____
Setting: _____

Favorite Part:

_____
_____
_____

Rating:
AWFUL
BAD
LAME
BORING
OKAY
NICE
GOOD
GREAT
SUPER
AMAZING

Draw or Copy an Illustration From Your Book:

Reading Time

Draw or Write About Four interesting Things From Your Book

Title:_____

Date:_____

Book of the Week

Choose your favorite book to focus on today. Choose a section to copy and after you're done, read it aloud seven times.

Title_____ Page Number_____

Story Board & Comics

Create a story board or comic strip based on
your favorite book from this week.

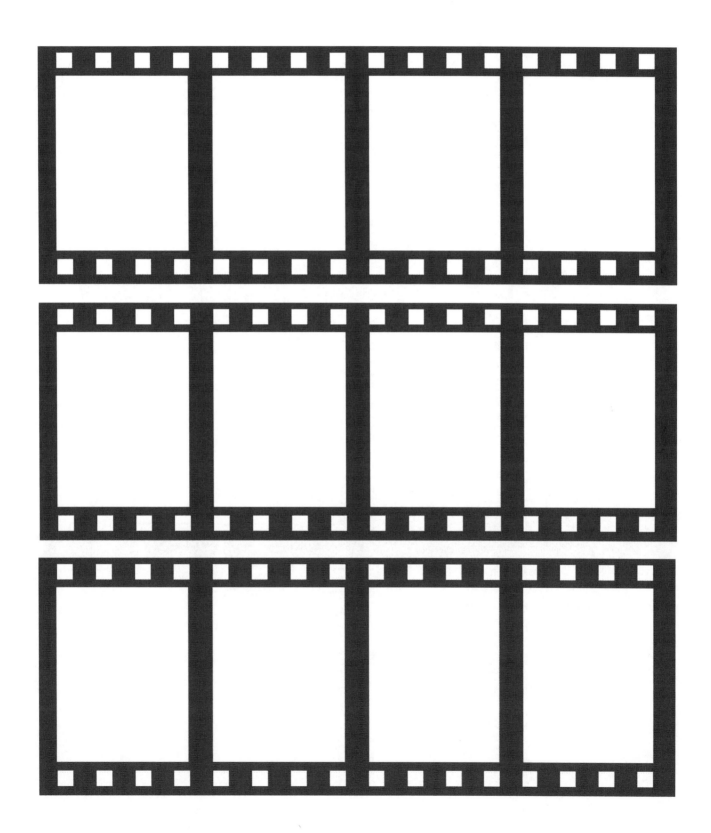

Journaling & Creative Writing

Date
_____

Book

Author: _____

Genre: _____

Illustrator: _____

Theme: _____

_____

Subject: _____
Setting: _____
Favorite Part:
_____
_____
_____

Rating:
AWFUL
BAD
LAME
BORING
OKAY
NICE
GOOD
GREAT
SUPER
AMAZING

Draw or Copy an Illustration From Your Book:

Reading Time

Draw or Write About Four interesting Things From Your Book

Title:_____

Date:_____

Date

Book

Author: _____

Genre: _____

Illustrator: _____

Theme: _____

_____

Subject: _____
Setting: _____

Favorite Part:

_____
_____
_____

Rating:
AWFUL
BAD
LAME
BORING
OKAY
NICE
GOOD
GREAT
SUPER
AMAZING

Draw or Copy an Illustration From Your Book:

Reading Time

Draw or Write About Four interesting Things From Your Book
Title:_____
Date:_____

Date

Book

Author: _____

Genre: _____

Illustrator: _____

Theme: _____

_____

Subject: _____
Setting: _____

Favorite Part:

_____
_____
_____

Rating:
AWFUL
BAD
LAME
BORING
OKAY
NICE
GOOD
GREAT
SUPER
AMAZING

Draw or Copy an Illustration From Your Book:

Words, Words, Words.

Write down ten words you liked from your reading time.
Using a thesaurus, look up related words and write them down too.

Thesaurus Words

WORD OF THE DAY:

What was your favorite word today and why?

Date

――――

Book

Author: _____

Genre: _____

Illustrator: _____

Theme: _____
_____

Subject: _____
Setting: _____

Favorite Part:
_____
_____
_____

Rating:
AWFUL
BAD
LAME
BORING
OKAY
NICE
GOOD
GREAT
SUPER
AMAZING

Draw or Copy an Illustration From Your Book:

Reading Time

Draw or Write About Four interesting Things From Your Book
Title:_____
Date:_____

Book of the Week

Choose your favorite book to focus on today. Choose a section to copy and after you're done, read it aloud seven times.

Title_____ Page Number_____

Story Board & Comics

Create a story board or comic strip based on your favorite book from this week.

Journaling & Creative Writing

Date

Book

Author: _____

Genre: _____

Illustrator: _____

Theme: _____

_____

Subject: _____
Setting: _____

Favorite Part:

_____
_____
_____

Rating:
AWFUL
BAD
LAME
BORING
OKAY
NICE
GOOD
GREAT
SUPER
AMAZING

Draw or Copy an Illustration From Your Book:

Reading Time

Draw or Write About Four interesting Things From Your Book

Title:_____

Date:_____

Date

Book

Author: _____

Genre: _____

Illustrator: _____

Theme: _____

_____

Subject: _____
Setting: _____

Favorite Part:
_____
_____
_____

Rating:
AWFUL
BAD
LAME
BORING
OKAY
NICE
GOOD
GREAT
SUPER
AMAZING

Draw or Copy an Illustration From Your Book:

Reading Time

Draw or Write About Four interesting Things From Your Book

Title:_____

Date:_____

Date

Book

Author: _____

Genre: _____

Illustrator: _____

Theme: _____

_____

Subject: _____
Setting: _____

Favorite Part:

_____
_____
_____

Rating:
AWFUL
BAD
LAME
BORING
OKAY
NICE
GOOD
GREAT
SUPER
AMAZING

Draw or Copy an Illustration From Your Book:

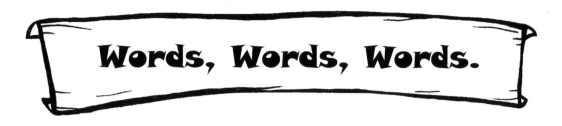

Words, Words, Words.

Write down ten words you liked from your reading time. Using a thesaurus, look up related words and write them down too.

Thesaurus Words

_____   _____

_____   _____

_____   _____

_____   _____

_____   _____

_____   _____

_____   _____

_____   _____

_____   _____

_____   _____

WORD OF THE DAY:

What was your favorite word today and why?

_____
_____
_____

Date

Book

Author: _____

Genre: _____

Illustrator: _____

Theme: _____

_____

Subject: _____
Setting: _____

Favorite Part:

_____
_____
_____

Rating:
AWFUL
BAD
LAME
BORING
OKAY
NICE
GOOD
GREAT
SUPER
AMAZING

Draw or Copy an Illustration From Your Book:

Reading Time

Draw or Write About Four interesting Things From Your Book

Title:_____

Date:_____

Choose your favorite book to focus on today. Choose a section to copy and after you're done, read it aloud seven times.

Title_____ Page Number_____

Story Board & Comics

Create a story board or comic strip based on your favorite book from this week.

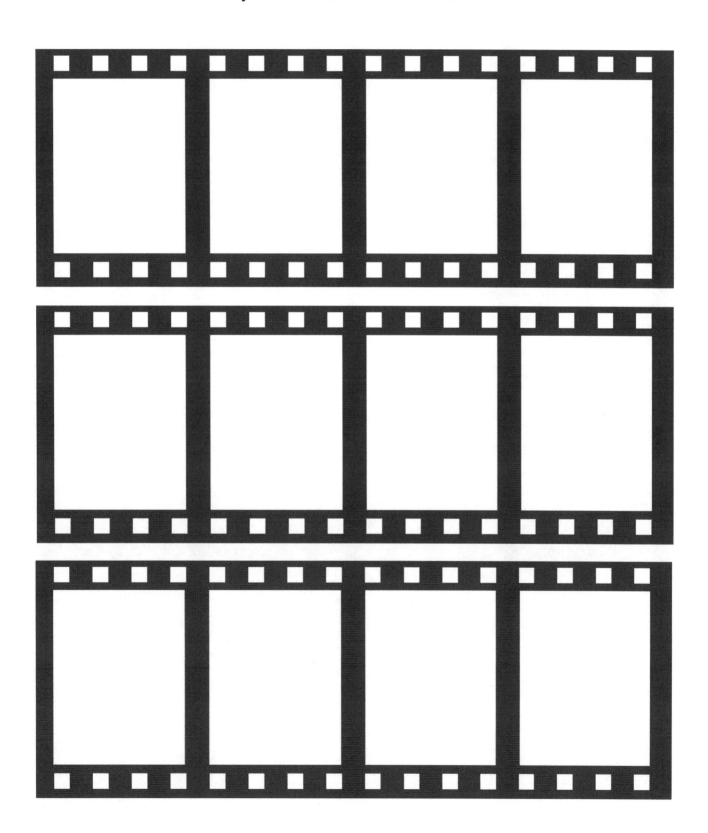

Journaling & Creative Writing

Date

_____

Book

Author: _____

Genre: _____

Illustrator: _____

Theme: _____

_____

Subject: _____
Setting: _____

Favorite Part:

_____
_____
_____

Rating:
AWFUL
BAD
LAME
BORING
OKAY
NICE
GOOD
GREAT
SUPER
AMAZING

Draw or Copy an Illustration From Your Book:

Reading Time

Draw or Write About Four interesting Things From Your Book
Title:_____
Date:_____

Date
_____

Book

Author: _____

Genre: _____

Illustrator: _____

Theme: _____
_____

Subject: _____
Setting: _____
Favorite Part:
_____
_____
_____

Rating:
AWFUL
BAD
LAME
BORING
OKAY
NICE
GOOD
GREAT
SUPER
AMAZING

Draw or Copy an Illustration From Your Book:

Reading Time

Draw or Write About Four interesting Things From Your Book

Title:_____

Date:_____

Date

Book

Author: _____

Genre: _____

Illustrator: _____

Theme: _____
_____

Subject: _____
Setting: _____

Favorite Part:

_____
_____
_____

Rating:
AWFUL
BAD
LAME
BORING
OKAY
NICE
GOOD
GREAT
SUPER
AMAZING

Draw or Copy an Illustration From Your Book:

Reading Time

Draw or Write About Four interesting Things From Your Book

Title:_____

Date:_____

Date

Book

Author: _____

Genre: _____

Illustrator: _____

Theme: _____

_____

Subject: _____
Setting: _____

Favorite Part:

_____
_____
_____

Rating:
AWFUL
BAD
LAME
BORING
OKAY
NICE
GOOD
GREAT
SUPER
AMAZING

Draw or Copy an Illustration From Your Book:

Reading Time

Draw or Write About Four interesting Things From Your Book

Title:_____

Date:_____

Choose your favorite book to focus on today. Choose a section to copy and after you're done, read it aloud seven times.

Title_____ Page Number_____

Story Board & Comics

Create a story board or comic strip based on your favorite book from this week.

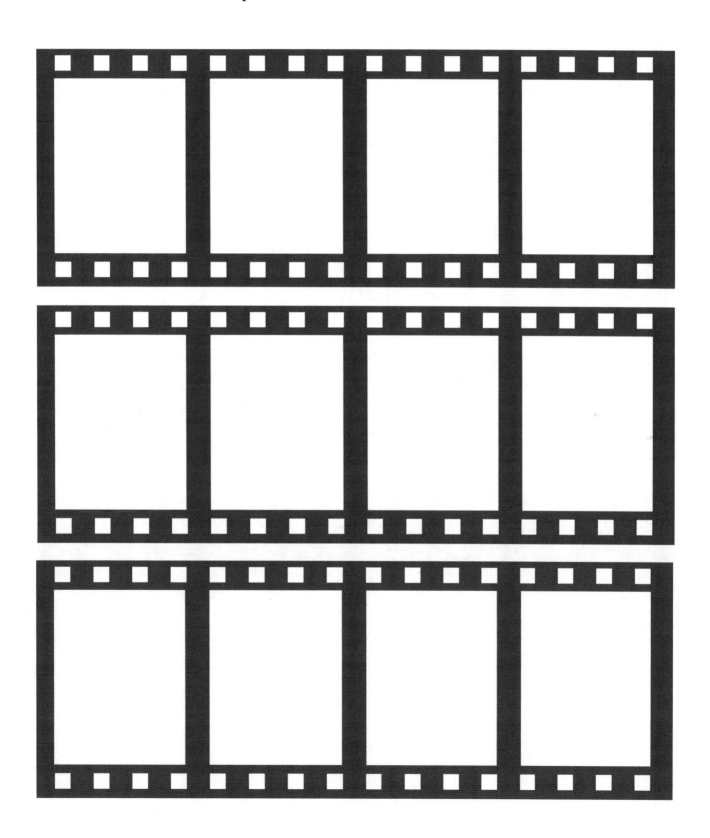

Journaling & Creative Writing

Date

Book

Author: _____

Genre: _____

Illustrator: _____

Theme: _____

_____

Subject: _____
Setting: _____

Favorite Part:

_____
_____
_____

Rating:
AWFUL
BAD
LAME
BORING
OKAY
NICE
GOOD
GREAT
SUPER
AMAZING

Draw or Copy an Illustration From Your Book:

Reading Time

Draw or Write About Four interesting Things From Your Book

Title:_____

Date:_____

Date

Book

Author: _____

Genre: _____

Illustrator: _____

Theme: _____

_____

Subject: _____
Setting: _____

Favorite Part:

_____
_____
_____

Rating:
AWFUL
BAD
LAME
BORING
OKAY
NICE
GOOD
GREAT
SUPER
AMAZING

Draw or Copy an Illustration From Your Book:

Reading Time

Draw or Write About Four interesting Things From Your Book

Title:_____

Date:_____

Date

Book

Author: _____

Genre: _____

Illustrator: _____

Theme: _____

_____

Subject: _____
Setting: _____

Favorite Part:
_____
_____
_____

Rating:
AWFUL
BAD
LAME
BORING
OKAY
NICE
GOOD
GREAT
SUPER
AMAZING

Draw or Copy an Illustration From Your Book:

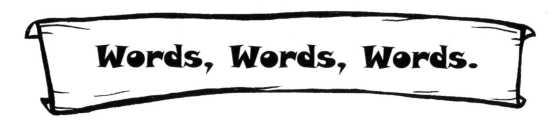
Words, Words, Words.

Write down ten words you liked from your reading time.
Using a thesaurus, look up related words and write them down too.

Thesaurus Words

WORD OF THE DAY:
What was your favorite word today and why?

Date

Book

Author: _____

Genre: _____

Illustrator: _____

Theme: _____

_____

Subject: _____
Setting: _____

Favorite Part:

_____

_____

_____

Rating:
AWFUL
BAD
LAME
BORING
OKAY
NICE
GOOD
GREAT
SUPER
AMAZING

Draw or Copy an Illustration From Your Book:

Reading Time

Draw or Write About Four interesting Things From Your Book

Title:_____

Date:_____

Choose your favorite book to focus on today. Choose a section to copy and after you're done, read it aloud seven times.

Title_____ Page Number_____

Story Board & Comics

Create a story board or comic strip based on
your favorite book from this week.

Journaling & Creative Writing

Date

Book

Author: _____

Genre: _____

Illustrator: _____

Theme: _____

_____

Subject: _____
Setting: _____

Favorite Part:

_____

_____

_____

Rating:
AWFUL
BAD
LAME
BORING
OKAY
NICE
GOOD
GREAT
SUPER
AMAZING

Draw or Copy an Illustration From Your Book:

Reading Time

Draw or Write About Four interesting Things From Your Book

Title:_____

Date:_____

Date
_____

Book

Author: _____

Genre: _____

Illustrator: _____

Theme: _____

_____

Subject: _____
Setting: _____

Favorite Part:

_____
_____
_____

Rating:
AWFUL
BAD
LAME
BORING
OKAY
NICE
GOOD
GREAT
SUPER
AMAZING

Draw or Copy an Illustration From Your Book:

Reading Time

Draw or Write About Four interesting Things From Your Book

Title:_____

Date:_____

Date

Book

Author: _____

Genre: _____

Illustrator: _____

Theme: _____
_____

Subject: _____
Setting: _____

Favorite Part:
_____
_____
_____

Rating:
AWFUL
BAD
LAME
BORING
OKAY
NICE
GOOD
GREAT
SUPER
AMAZING

Draw or Copy an Illustration From Your Book:

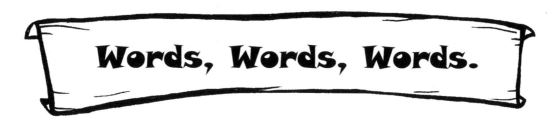

Words, Words, Words.

Write down ten words you liked from your reading time.
Using a thesaurus, look up related words and write them down too.

Thesaurus Words

_____   _____
_____   _____
_____   _____
_____   _____
_____   _____
_____   _____
_____   _____
_____   _____
_____   _____
_____   _____
_____   _____
_____   _____

WORD OF THE DAY:

What was your favorite word today and why?

_____
_____

Date

Book

Author: _____

Genre: _____

Illustrator: _____

Theme: _____

_____

Subject: _____
Setting: _____

Favorite Part:

_____
_____
_____

Rating:
AWFUL
BAD
LAME
BORING
OKAY
NICE
GOOD
GREAT
SUPER
AMAZING

Draw or Copy an Illustration From Your Book:

Reading Time

Draw or Write About Four interesting Things From Your Book

Title:_____

Date:_____

Book of the Week

Choose your favorite book to focus on today. Choose a section to copy and after you're done, read it aloud seven times.

Title_____ Page Number_____

Story Board & Comics

Create a story board or comic strip based on your favorite book from this week.

Journaling & Creative Writing

Journaling & Creative Writing

Date

Book

Author: _____

Genre: _____

Illustrator: _____

Theme: _____

_____

Subject: _____
Setting: _____

Favorite Part:

_____
_____
_____

Rating:
AWFUL
BAD
LAME
BORING
OKAY
NICE
GOOD
GREAT
SUPER
AMAZING

Draw or Copy an Illustration From Your Book:

Reading Time

Draw or Write About Four interesting Things From Your Book

Title:_____

Date:_____

Date
_____

Book

Author: _____

Genre: _____

Illustrator: _____

Theme: _____

_____

Subject: _____
Setting: _____

Favorite Part:

_____
_____
_____

Rating:
AWFUL
BAD
LAME
BORING
OKAY
NICE
GOOD
GREAT
SUPER
AMAZING

Draw or Copy an Illustration From Your Book:

Reading Time

Draw or Write About Four interesting Things From Your Book

Title:_____

Date:_____

Date

Book

Author: _____

Genre: _____

Illustrator: _____

Theme: _____

_____

Subject: _____
Setting: _____

Favorite Part:

_____
_____
_____

Rating:
AWFUL
BAD
LAME
BORING
OKAY
NICE
GOOD
GREAT
SUPER
AMAZING

Draw or Copy an Illustration From Your Book:

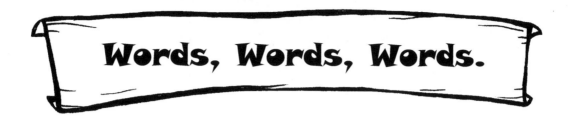

Words, Words, Words.

Write down ten words you liked from your reading time.
Using a thesaurus, look up related words and write them down too.

Thesaurus Words

_____   _____
_____   _____
_____   _____
_____   _____
_____   _____
_____   _____
_____   _____
_____   _____
_____   _____
_____   _____

WORD OF THE DAY:
What was your favorite word today and why?

_____
_____

Date

Book

Author: _____

Genre: _____

Illustrator: _____

Theme: _____

_____

Subject: _____
Setting: _____

Favorite Part:

_____
_____
_____

Rating:
AWFUL
BAD
LAME
BORING
OKAY
NICE
GOOD
GREAT
SUPER
AMAZING

Draw or Copy an Illustration From Your Book:

Reading Time

Draw or Write About Four interesting Things From Your Book

Title:_____

Date:_____

Book of the Week

Choose your favorite book to focus on today. Choose a section to copy and after you're done, read it aloud seven times.

Title_____ Page Number_____

Story Board & Comics

Create a story board or comic strip based on your favorite book from this week.

Journaling & Creative Writing

Journaling & Creative Writing

Made in the USA
Middletown, DE
03 July 2024

56802379R00104